VOCAL SELECTIONS From MAME

Music and Lyrics by JERRY HERMAN

COLUMBIA ORIGINAL CAST ALBUM

A PUBLICATION OF
EDWIN H. MORRIS & COMPANY
A DIVISION OF
MPL COMMUNICATIONS, INC.
http://www.mplcommunications.com

EXCLUSIVELY DISTRIBUTED BY
HAL•LEONARD® CORPORATION
7777 W. BLUEMOUND RD. P.O. BOX 13819 MILWAUKEE, WI 53213

St. Bridget

From the Broadway Musical "MAME"

Music and Lyrics by
JERRY HERMAN

Slowly, with expression

SAINT BRIDG - ET, de - liv - er us to Beek-man Place, A-

way from the wick - ed and de - praved;

gray head is peep - ing through the cur - tain lace, Call - ing

"Come ye in - side, where you'll be saved." She's

It's Today

From the Broadway Musical "MAME"

Music and Lyrics by
JERRY HERMAN

Brightly, in 2

Piano

Chorus

1. Light the can - dles, _____ Get the
(2. Light the) can - dles, _____ Fill the

ice out, _____ Roll the rug up, _____
punch bowl, _____ Throw con - fet - ti, _____

"OPEN A NEW WINDOW"

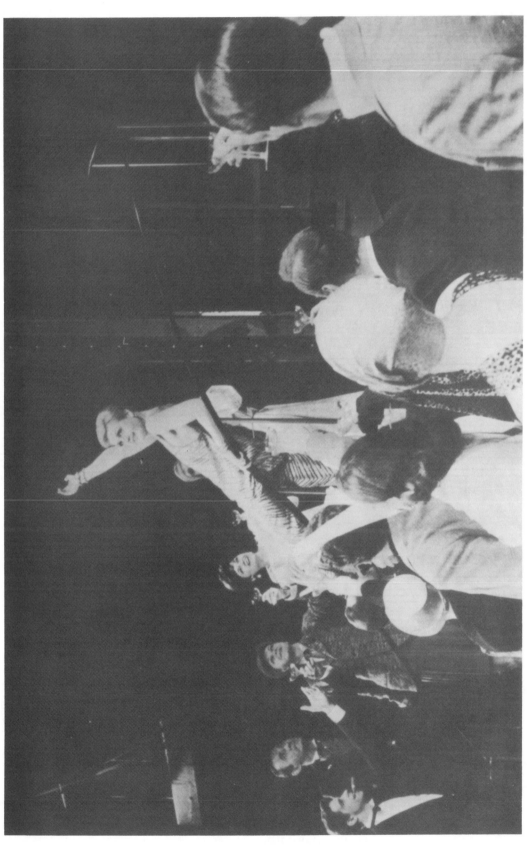

Open A New Window

From the Broadway Musical "MAME"

Music and Lyrics by
JERRY HERMAN

March tempo

Piano

Chorus

O - PEN A NEW WIN - DOW, O - pen a new door,

Trav - el a new high - way, that's nev - er been tried be - fore; Be - fore you

The Man In The Moon

From the Broadway Musical "MAME"

Music and Lyrics by
JERRY HERMAN

BEATRICE ARTHUR

"THE MAN IN THE MOON"

My Best Girl
(My Best Beau)
From the Broadway Musical "MAME"

Music and Lyrics by
JERRY HERMAN

We Need A Little Christmas

From the Broadway Musical "MAME"

Music and Lyrics by
JERRY HERMAN

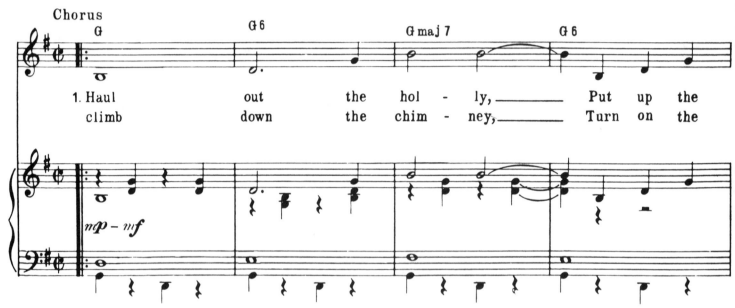

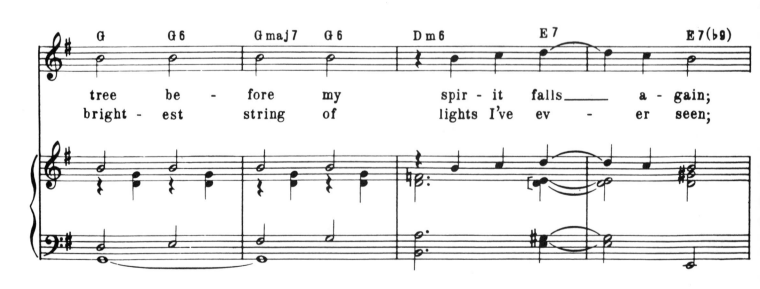

Mame

From the Broadway Musical "MAME"

Music and Lyrics by
JERRY HERMAN

ANGELA LANSBURY and FRANKIE MICHAELS

"MAME"

"WE NEED A LITTLE CHRISTMAS"

Bosom Buddies

From the Broadway Musical "MAME"

Music and Lyrics by
JERRY HERMAN

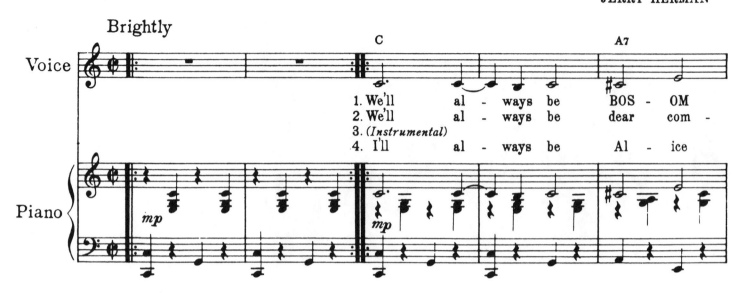

Brightly

1. We'll al - ways be BOS - OM
2. We'll al - ways be dear com -
3. (Instrumental)
4. I'll al - ways be Al - ice

BUD - DIES, friends, sis - ters and pals;
pan - ions, my cro - ny, my mate;
Tok - las, if you'll be Ger - trude Stein.

We'll al - ways be BOS - OM BUD - DIES, If life should re - ject
We'll al - ways be har - mo - niz - ing, Or - phan An - nie and Sand -
And tho' I'll ad - mit I've dished you, I've gos - siped and gloat -

34

"BOSOM BUDDIES"

Gooch's Song

From the Broadway Musical "MAME"

Music and Lyrics by
JERRY HERMAN

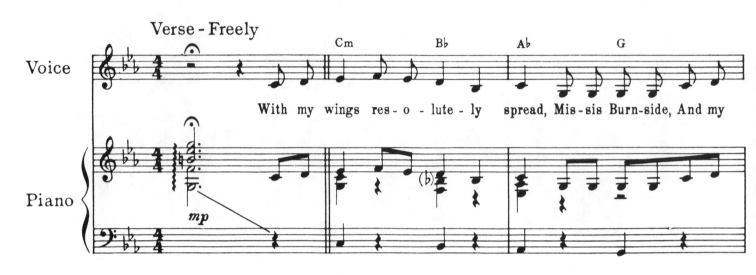

With my wings res-o-lute-ly spread, Mis-sis Burn-side, And my

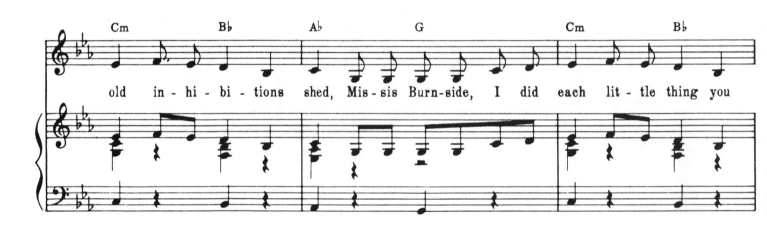

old in-hi-bi-tions shed, Mis-sis Burn-side, I did each lit-tle thing you

said, Mis-sis Burn-side, I lived! I lived! I lived! I

Chorus - Moderato (*not too fast*)

That's How Young I Feel

From the Broadway Musical "MAME"

Music and Lyrics by
JERRY HERMAN

If He Walked Into My Life

From the Broadway Musical "MAME"

Music and Lyrics by
JERRY HERMAN